MW01503390

U.K. DVSA

HIGHWAY CODE TEST

QUESTIONS & ANSWERS

REVISED EDITION

Over 200 Drivers Test Questions for the U.K.
Drivers Theory Test for 2021 to 2023

John B. Blackwell

Copyright

Table of content

CHAPTER ONE--**4**

PRACTICE THEORY TESTS---**4**

  MOCK THEORY TEST 1---**4**

  MOCK THEORY TEST 2-- **20**

CHAPTER TWO --- **47**

HIGHWAY CODE STUDY TESTS------------------------------- **47**

  (Alertness, Distractions, Mirrors, and Blind Spots Tests) 47

CHAPTER THREE --- **62**

RULES OF THE ROAD -- **62**

CHAPTER FOUR-- **80**

ROAD SIGNS TEST--- **80**

FREQUENTLY ASKED QUESTIONS ----------------------- **106**

  What is the minimum age requirement for the tests? --- **106**

  How can I request for my theory test? ---------------------- **106**

  What does the theory tests constitute? ---------------------- **106**

  What am I required to study? --------------------------------- **107**

  Where are these questions from ?----------------------------- **107**

CHAPTER ONE

PRACTICE THEORY TESTS

MOCK THEORY TEST 1

(29 Test Questions and Answers)

1.   When are you required to use hazard warning lights?

a)   When stationary and temporarily obstructing traffic

b)   When driving during darkness without headlights

c)   When you are parked for shopping on double yellow lines

d)   When driving slowly because you are lost

Answer: A

2. What are triangular signs used for?

a) To give warnings

b) To give information

c) To give orders

d) To give directions

Answer: B

3. **What is the meaning of the below sign?**

a) Change to the left lane

b) Leave at the next exit

c) Contra flow system

d) One-way street

Answer: C

4. **When driving without insurance, you will be fined a maximum of?**

a) £50

b) £500

c) £1,000

d) £5,000

Answer: D

5. **A heavy load on your vehicles' roof rack will definitely do what?**

a) improve the road holding

b) reduce the stopping distance

c) make the steering lighter

d) reduce stability

Answer: C

6. **When you park your vehicle at night on a road with a 40 mph speed limit. You are required to park**

a) facing the traffic

b) with parking lights on

c) with dipped headlights on

d) near a street light

Answer: B

7. **When you want to turn right at a box junction, and there is an oncoming traffic. You are required to**

a) Stay in the box junction if your exit is clear

b) Stop before the junction until it is clear of all traffic

c) Move on, you cannot turn right at a box junction

d) Travel slowly into the box junction when signalled by approaching traffic.

Answer: B

8. **What is the right-hand lane meant for on a three-lane motorway?**

a) For emergency vehicles only

b) For overtaking

c) For vehicles towing trailers

d) For coaches only

Answer: B

9. **You are on a motorway, and a 'Red Cross' is displayed above the shoulder. What does this supposed to mean?**

a) Stop in this lane to answer your mobile phone

b) Use this lane as a running lane

c) This lane can be used if you need a rest

d) You should not travel in this lane

Answer: D

10. **You are on a motorway at night with other vehicles in front of your vehicle. Which lights should you switch on?**

a) Front fog lights

b) Main beam headlights

c) Sidelights only

d) Dipped headlights

Answer: **D**

11. **You may use your vehicle's front fog lights with headlights, if the visibility is reduced to less than what metres?**

a) 100 metres (328 feet)

b) 200 metres (656 feet)

c) 300 metres (984 feet)

d) 400 metres (1312 feet)

Answer: **A**

12. **If you are driving behind a long lorry, and the driver signals to turn left onto a narrow road. What should you do?**

a) Overtake on the left before the lorry reaches the junction

b) Overtake on the right as soon as the lorry slows down

c) Do not overtake unless you can see there is no oncoming traffic

d) Do not overtake. Stay well back and be prepared to stop

Answer: D

13. **It is very windy, and you are behind a motorcyclist who is overtaking a high-sided vehicle. What are you supposed to do?**

a) Overtake the motorcyclist immediately

b) Keep well back

c) Stay level with the motorcyclist

d) Keep close to the motorcyclist

Answer: B

14. **You are turning left from a main road into a side road, and pedestrians are already crossing the road into which you are turning. You should then do what?**

a) continue, as it is your right of way

b) signal to them to continue crossing

c) wait and allow them to cross

d) sound your horn to warn them of your presence

Answer: C

15. **Motorcyclists are required to often look round over their right shoulder just before turning right. This is because**

a) they need to listen very well for following traffic

b) not all motorcycles have mirrors

c) doing so makes them stable as they turn

d) they suppose to look out for traffic in their blind area

Answer: D

16. **Whenever you sight this sign ahead. You should expect the road to**

a) go steeply uphill

b) go steeply downhill

c) bend sharply to the left

d) bend sharply to the right

Answer: C

17. **When you are trailing a slow moving vehicle on a narrow country road and there is a junction just ahead on the right. What are you to do?**

a) Overtake after checking your mirrors and signalling

b) Stay behind until you are past the junction

c) Accelerate quickly to pass before the junction

d) Slow down and prepare to overtake on the left

Answer: B

18. **Braking distances when driving on icy road can be**

a)   twice the normal distance

b)   five times the normal distance

c)   seven times the normal distance

d)   ten times the normal distance

Answer: **D**

19. **The overall stopping distance comprises of thinking and braking distances respectively. You are on a dry road with good brakes and tyres. What is the actual BRAKING distance from 50 mph?**

a)   14 metres (46 feet)

b)   24 metres (80 feet)

c)   38 metres (125 feet)

d)   55 metres (180 feet)

Answer: **C**

20. **When your tyres are under-inflated, one of the following is badly affected**

a) Braking

b) Indicating

c) Changing gear

d) Parking

Answer: A

21. **Why you are not supposed to wave people across at pedestrian crossing is because**

a) there may be another vehicle coming

b) they may not be looking

c) it is safer for you to carry on

d) they may not be ready to cross

Answer: A

22. When you are approaching a pelican crossing and the amber light is flashing. What must you do?

a) give way to pedestrians who are crossing

b) encourage pedestrians to cross

c) not move until the green light appears

d) stop even if the crossing is clear

Answer: A

23. Which of the under listed may cause loss of concentration when driving on a long journey?

a) Keeping fresh air circulating

b) Arguing with a passenger

c) Stopping regularly to rest

d) Pulling up to tune the radio

Answer: B

24. When you are driving and your mobile phone rings, you are required to do what before answering it?

a) reduce your speed to 30 mph

b) pull up on the hard shoulder

c) move into the left-hand lane

d) stop in a safe place

Answer: D

25. When is it advisable to drive a motor car in the bus lane

a) Outside its hours of operation

b) To move to the front of a traffic gridlock

c) You may not use it at any time

d) To overtake slow-moving traffic

Answer: A

26. **Before driving anyone else's motor vehicle you are required to make sure that?**

a) the owner of the vehicle has third party insurance cover

b) your vehicle has insurance cover

c) the vehicle is as a matter of fact insured for your use

d) the owner of the vehicle has left the insurance documents in the vehicle

Answer: C

27. **which condition should you NOT proceed when the light is green**

a) When pedestrians are waiting to cross the road

b) When your exit from the junction is blocked by other road users

c) When you think the lights is about to change

d) When you plan to make a right turn

Answer: B

28. You are driving on a motorway. Unless there is a road sign showing a lower speed limit, your travelling speed must NOT exceed

a) 50 mile per hour

b) 60 mile per hour

c) 70 mile per hour

d) 80 mile per hour

Answer: C

29. What is the importance of painting place names on road surfaces?

a) To limit traffic flow

b) To warn road users of oncoming traffic

c) To enable drivers to change lanes early

d) To prevent drivers from changing lanes

Answer: C

MOCK THEORY TEST 2

(50 Test Questions and Answers)

1. **You are driving behind a bus and it suddenly pulls up at a bus stop. What are you required to do?**

a) Accelerate past the bus

b) Watch carefully for pedestrians

c) Sound your horn

d) Pull in closely behind the bus

Answer: B

2. **Why is it bad technique to speed whilst driving downhill?**

a) The fuel consumption will increase

b) The engine will overheat

c) The tyres will wear more quickly

d) The vehicle will gain speed

Answer: D

3. **As you are driving on a two-lane dual carriageway highway. Why then would you use the right-hand lane?**

a) To overtake slower traffic

b) For normal progress

c) When maintaining the minimum allowed speed

d) To keep travelling at a steady high speed

Answer: A

4. **What does the third party insurance cover?**

a) Damage to your vehicle

b) Fire damage to your vehicle

c) Flood damage to your vehicle

d) Damage to other vehicles by you

Answer: D

5. **Which document are you to provide for the police when you are involved in a collision?**

a) Vehicle registration document

b) Driver's licence

c) Theory test certificate

d) Vehicle service record

Answer: B

6. **Which of the following is required before you can drive legally in the U.K?**

a) A vehicle handbook

b) Proper insurance cover

c) A vehicle service record

d) Breakdown cover

Answer: B

7. **At puffin crossings, which light will a driver not certainly?**

a) Flashing amber

b) Red

c) Steady amber

d) Green

Answer: A

8. **As you are approaching a right-hand bend why should you keep well to the left?**

a) To improve your view of the road

b) To find a way through the effect of the road's slope

c) To let faster traffic from behind overtake

d) To be positioned safely if you skid

Answer: A

9. **What should you do when turning right into a dual Carriageway?**

a) Stop your vehicle and apply the handbrake and then select a low gear

b) Make sure that your vehicle is well positioned to the left of the side road

c) Confirm that the central reservation is wide enough for your vehicle

d) Make sure there is enough room for the vehicle following you.

Answer: C

10. **In which of the following should overtaking be avoided?**

a) Just after a bend

b) In a one-way street

c) On a 30 mph road

d) When approaching a dip in the road

Answer: D

11. **Which colour follows the green signal at a puffing crossing?**

a) Steady red

b) Flashing amber

c) Steady amber

d) Flashing green

Answer: C

12. **To avoid dazzling following drivers on a traffic queue at night, you should do what?**

a) apply the handbrake only

b) apply the footbrake only

c) switch off your headlights

d) use both the handbrake and footbrake

Answer: A

13. **What is the percentage of emissions caused by road transport?**

a)   10%

b)   20%

c)   30%

d)   40%

Answer: B

14. **When the wheels on a car are unbalanced it may cause what?**

a)   the steering to pull to one side

b)   the steering to vibrate

c)   the brakes to fail

d)   the tyres to deflate

Answer: B

15. **What is the typical overall stopping distance when driving at a speed of 50mph on a good, dry road?**

a) 36 metres (118 feet)

b) 53 metres (175 feet)

c) 75 metres (245 feet)

d) 96 metres (315 feet)

Answer: B

16. **What is the typical overall stopping distance when driving at a speed of 40mph on a good, dry road?**

a) 23 metres (75 feet)

b) 36 metres (118 feet)

c) 53 metres (175 feet)

d) 96 metres (315 feet)

Answer: B

17. What would be the first warning of an approaching train when you are travelling towards the below shown level crossing?

a) Both half barriers down

b) A steady amber light

c) One half barrier down

d) Twin flashing red lights

Answer: B

18. **What is the meaning of the below signal by the police Officer shown below?**

a) Go ahead

b) Stop

c) Turn left

d) Turn right

Answer: B

19. What does the below sign mean?

a) Contra flow pedal cycle lane

b) With-flow pedal cycle lane

c) Pedal cycles and buses only

d) No pedal cycles or buses

Answer: B

20. **When you see a pedestrian with a dog putting on a yellow or burgundy coat. This warns you that the pedestrian is what?**

a) elderly

b) dog training

c) colour blind

d) deaf

Answer: D

21. **You are waiting to emerge left from a minor road and suddenly a large vehicle is approaching you from the right. Why should you wait?**

a) The large vehicle can easily your view of an overtaking vehicle

b)   The large vehicle can turn without suddenly warning

c)   The large vehicle is difficult to manoeuvre in a straight line

d)   The large vehicle can easily hide vehicles coming from the left

Answer: A

22. **Which of the following is most likely not to be affected by crosswinds**

a)   Cyclists

b)   Motorcyclists

c)   High-sided vehicles

d)   Cars

Answer: D

23. **When can you to overtake another vehicle on the left side?**

a)   When you're in a one-way street

b)   When approaching a junction where you'll be turning off

c)   When the vehicle in front is signalling to turn left

d) When a slower moving vehicle is travelling in the right-hand lane of a dual carriageway

Answer: A

24. When your vehicle begins to skid on a wet road as a result of the application of brakes. What should be the first thing to do?

a) Quickly pull up the handbrake

b) Release the footbrake

c) Push harder on the brake pedal

d) Gently use the accelerator

Answer: B

25. Which of the following is used to reduce traffic bunching on a motorway?

a) Variable speed limits

b) Contra flow systems

c) National speed limits

d) Lane closures

Answer: A

26. **When there is a red flashing light above every lane on a motorway, you must**

a) pull onto the hard shoulder

b) slow down and watch for further signals

c) leave at the next exit

d) stop and wait

Answer: D

27. **If you are driving at night with full beam headlights on, and a vehicle is overtaking you, when are you supposed to dip your lights?**

a) A little time after the vehicle has passed you

b) Prior to the vehicle passing you

c) only if the other driver dips his/her headlights

d) as soon as the vehicle passes you

Answer: D

28. You may park your vehicle on the right-hand side of a road at night

a) in a one-way street

b) with your sidelights on

c) not less than 11 metres from a junction

d) under a lamp-post

Answer: A

29. What does the below sign represent?

a) Waiting restrictions apply

b) Waiting permitted

c) National speed limit applies

d) Clearway (no stopping)

Answer: A

29. What is the meaning of the sign below?

a) End of restricted speed area

b) End of restricted parking area

c) End of clearway

d) End of cycle route

Answer: B

30. What is the period of validity for Statutory off Road Notification (SORN)?

a) Unless the vehicle is taxed, sold or scrapped.

b) Unless the vehicle is insured and MOT'd.

c) Unless the vehicle is repaired or modified.

d) Unless the vehicle is used on the road

Answer: A

31. Unless your vehicle have current MOT certificate, you may not be able to

a) Renew your driving licence

b) Change your insurance company

c) Renew your vehicle excise licence

d) Notify a change of address

Answer: C

32. When you arrive at an incident scene where there has been an engine fire and someone's hands and arms

have been burnt, you are required not to do one of the following?

a) douse the burn thoroughly with clean cool non-toxic liquid

b) lay the casualty down on the ground

c) remove anything sticking to the burn

d) reassure them confidently and repeatedly

Answer: C

33. **What should you do in case of an incident that involves casualties?**

a) get them out of the vehicle

b) give them a drink

c) give them something to eat

d) keep them in the vehicle

Answer: D

34. When you are towing a small trailer on a busy three-lane motorway in which all the lanes are open, YOU MUST

a)   not exceed 50 mph

b)   not overtake

c)   have a stabiliser fitted

d)   use only the left and centre lanes

Answer: D

35. What additional safety device can be fitted to the trailer braking system apart from securely hitching up the trailer to the towing vehicle

a)   Stabiliser

b)   Jockey wheel

c)   Corner steadies

d)   Breakaway cable

Answer: D

36. You are driving behind a large vehicle approaching crossroads and suddenly the driver signals to turn left. What are you required to do?

a) Overtake when there are no oncoming vehicles

b) Do not overtake until the vehicle begins to turn

c) Never overtake when at or approaching a junction

d) Overtake when there are oncoming vehicles

Answer: C

37. If you are to park on the road at night, where is it mandatory for you to use parking lights?

a) Where there are continuous white lines in the centre of the road

b) Where the speed limit exceeds 30 mph

c) Where you are facing oncoming traffic

d) Where you are near a bus stop

Answer: B

38. How should you position your vehicle if you are to turn right into a one – way street?

a) In the right-hand lane

b) In the left-hand lane

c) In either lane, depending on the traffic

d) Just left of the centre line

Answer: A

39. What should you do when following a motorcyclist on an uneven road?

a) Adjust accordingly so you can be seen in their mirrors

b) Overtake as soon as possible

c) Give extra room in case they swerve, to avoid potholes

d) Give the same room as normal because road surfaces do not affect motorcyclists

Answer: C

40. What should you do when driving at night behind another vehicle in an unlit road?

a) Flash your headlights

b) Use dipped beam headlights

c) Switch off your headlights

d) Use full beam headlights

Answer: B

41. **How is a 30 mph limit indicated when there are no Speed limit signs on a road?**

    a) By hazard warning lines

    b) By street lighting

    c) By pedestrian islands

    d) By double or single yellow lines

    Answer: B

42. **What are you supposed to do: to control the speed limit of your vehicle when going down a steep?**

    a) Adjust to a high gear and use the brakes carefully

    b) Adjust to a high gear and use the brakes firmly

    c) Adjust to a low gear and use the brakes carefully

    d) Adjust to a low gear and avoid using the brakes

    Answer: C

43. **What is the national designed speed limit for vehicles and motorcycles in the middle lane of a three- lane motorway?**

    a) 40 mph

    b) 50 mph

    c) 60 mph

    d) 70 mph

Answer: D

44. In windy conditions, you are required to take very good care when

a) Using the brakes

b) Making a hill start

c) Turning into a narrow road

d) Passing pedal cyclists

Answer: D

45. Your vehicle broke down on a motorway and you are unable to stop on the hard shoulder. What should you do?

a) Switch on your hazard warning lights

b) Stop following traffic and ask for help

c) Attempt to repair your vehicle quickly

d) Stand behind your vehicle to warn others

Answer: A

46. What do circular traffic sign with a blue background like the one shown below signify?

a)   Give warning regarding a motorway ahead

b)   Give direction for a car park

c)   Give information about a motorway

d)   Give an instruction

Answer: D

47. When might you be allowed to wait in a yellow box junction?

a)   Oncoming traffic is preventing you from turning right

b)   You are in a queue of traffic turning left

c)   You are in a queue of traffic to go ahead

d)   You are on a roundabout

Answer: A

48. **Why is it dangerous keeping the clutch down or selecting neutral for long periods of time?**

    a) Fuel spillage may occur

    b) It may result in engine damage

    c) It will cause less steering and braking control

    d) It will wear tyres out more quickly

    Answer: C

49. **What minimum time gap should you give if you are following a vehicle on a wet road?**

    a) One second

    b) Two seconds

    c) Three seconds

    d) Four seconds

    Answer: D

50. **You have been travelling with your car in thick fog which has now cleared. Why must you switch OFF your rear fog lights?**

    a) They use a lot of power from the battery

    b) They make your brake lights less clear

    c) They will cause dazzles in your rear view mirrors

d) They may not be properly adjusted

Answer: B

CHAPTER TWO

HIGHWAY CODE STUDY TESTS

(Alertness, Distractions, Mirrors, and Blind Spots Tests)

(36 Questions and Answers)

1. **You are driving along this narrow country road. When passing the cyclist you should move**

a) slowly, sounding the horn as you pass

b) quickly, leaving plenty of room

c)   slowly, leaving plenty of room

d)   quickly, sounding the horn as you pass

Answer: C

2.   **What should you do when your mobile phone rings as you are driving?**

a)   stop immediately

b)   answer it immediately

c)   pull up in a suitable place

d)   pull up at the nearest kerb

Answer: C

3.   **If your vehicle is fitted with a hand-held telephone, to make use of the telephone you should**

a)   reduce your speed

b)   find a safe place to stop

c)   steer the vehicle with one hand

d)   be particularly careful at junctions

Answer: B

4.   **When emerging from junctions as you are driving, one of the following is most likely to obstruct your view?**

a)   Windscreen pillars

b) Steering wheel

c) Interior mirror

d) Windscreen wipers

Answer: A

5. **When your view is obstructed by parked vehicles as you are waiting to turn right at the end of a road, what are you required to do?**

a) Stop your vehicle, and then proceed slowly and carefully for a proper view

b) Proceed quickly to where you can see so you only block traffic from one direction

c) Wait for a pedestrian to let you know when it is safe for you to proceed

d) Turn your vehicle around as soon as possible and find another junction to use

Answer: A

6. What are you required to do: as you approach this bridge shown below?

a) move to the right

b) slow down

c) change gear

d) keep to 30 mph

Answer: B

7. **Which of the following should you do when moving off from behind a parked car?**

a) give a signal after moving off

b) check both interior and exterior mirrors

c) look round after moving off

d) use the exterior mirrors only

Answer: B

8. **When you are approaching traffic lights that have been showing green for some time, you should**

a) accelerate hard

b) maintain your speed

c) be ready to stop

d) brake hard

Answer: C

9. **Why are you required to use the mirrors when you see a hazard ahead of you?**

a) Because you will need to speed out of danger

b) To observe how your actions will affect following traffic

c) Because you will need to stop immediately

d) To view what is happening on the road ahead

Answer: B

10. **When using hands-free phone as you are driving, it is likely to**

a) improve your safety

b) increase your concentration

c) reduce your view

d) divert your attention

Answer: D

11. **How should you avoid been distracted while driving, if your car is equipped with a navigation system?**

a) Keep driving and input your destination into the system

b) Keep driving as the system will adjust to your route

c) Come to a stop to view and use the system

d) Come to a stop in a safe place before using the system

Answer: D

12. **When is the most suitable time to use a mobile phone?**

a) When receiving a call

b) When suitably parked

c) When driving at less than 30 mph

d) When driving an automatic vehicle

Answer: B

13. Which of the following should you be particularly aware of when waiting to emerge from a junction and the windscreen pillars is restricting your view

a) Lorries

b) Buses

c) Motorcyclists

d) Coaches

Answer: C

14. What is the meaning of "blind spot" to a driver?

a) An area covered by your right-hand mirror

b) An area not covered by your headlights

c) An area covered by your left-hand mirror

d) An area not covered by your mirrors

Answer: D

15. Why are yellow lines painted across some roads?

a) To help you choose the correct lane

b) To help the motorist to keep to the correct separation distance

c) To make you aware of how fast or slow you are travelling

d) To tell you the distance to the roundabout ahead

Answer: C

16. One of the following is why a driver should keep well back while following a large vehicle

a) To allows you to corner more quickly

b) To helps the large vehicle to stop more easily

c) To allows the driver to see you in the mirrors

d) To helps you to keep out of the wind

Answer: C

17. What is the best action to take when you lose your way on a busy road?

a) Come to a stop at traffic lights and ask pedestrians for direction

b) Shout to other drivers to enquire about the way to go

c) Turn into a side road, stop your vehicle and then check a map

d) Check a map, and keep driving with the traffic flow

Answer: C

18. You are driving on a wet road and suddenly you have to stop in an emergency. You should then

a) apply the handbrake and footbrake together

b) keep both hands on the wheel

c) select reverse gear

d) give an arm signal

Answer: B

19. What are you required to do prior to making a U turn?

a) Use an arm signal as well as using your indicators

b) Check road markings to see that U-turns are legal

c) Look over your shoulder to make sure that all is clear

d) Adjust to a higher gear than normal

Answer: C

20. Which of the under listed are you supposed to do, prior to stopping?

a) Sound the horn

b) Use the mirrors

c) Select a higher gear

d) Flash your headlights

Answer: B

21. **You are travelling at the legal speed limit and suddenly a vehicle approaches up quickly behind, with its headlights flashing. What should you do?**

a) Speed up to make a gap behind you

b) apply the brakes sharply to show your brake lights

c) keep your speed constant to prevent the vehicle from overtaking

d) allow the vehicle to overtake yours

   Answer: **D**

22. **What is your vehicle horn meant for?**

a) To alert others of your presence

b) To allow you right of way

c) To greet other road users

d) To signal your annoyance

   Answer: **A**

23. **When you are driving along a country road and a horse rider is approaching. What are you required to do?**

a) Increase your speed

b) Sound your horn

c) Flash your headlights

d) Drive slowly past

Answer: D

24. **You are approaching a red light at a puffin crossing, and pedestrians are on the crossing. The red light will keep on until**

a) you start to move slightly forward on to the crossing

b) the pedestrians have reached a safe position

c) the pedestrians are clear of the front of your vehicle

d) vehicle from the opposite direction reaches the crossing

Answer: B

25. **At a pelican crossing, when the amber light is flashing, it means you MUST**

a) stop and wait for the green light

b) stop and wait for the red light

c) yield to pedestrians waiting to cross

d) yield to pedestrians already on the crossing

Answer: D

26. **When a bus lane on your left shows no times of operation. It means it is**

a) not in operation at all

b) only in operation at peak times

c) in operation 24 hours a day

d) only in operation in daylight hours

Answer: C

27. At which type of the following crossing are cyclists permitted to ride across with pedestrians?

a) Toucan

b) Puffin

c) Pelican

d) Zebra

Answer: A

28. Which of following services' personnel can display a blue flashing beacon?

a) Coastguard

b) Doctor's car

c) Gritting lorry

d) Animal ambulance

Answer: A

29. Which of the below depicted instrument panel warning light shows that headlights are on full beam?

a)

b)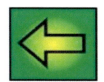

c)

d)

Answer: A

30. One of the following is an advantage you will get by taking part in the Pass Plus scheme?

a) never get any points on your licence

b) be able to service your own car

c) allow you to drive anyone else's vehicle

d) improve your basic driving skills

Answer: D

31. One of the following documents is a necessity when you want to apply for renewal of your vehicle excise licence?

a) Valid insurance.

b) The chassis number.

c) The handbook.

d) A valid driving licence

Answer: A

32. For how long will an MOT certificate remain valid?

a) three years after the date it was issued

b) 10,000 miles

c) one year after the date it was issued

d) 30,000 miles

Answer: C

33. It is a MUST for a newly qualified driver to

a) display green 'L' plates

b) not exceed 40 mph for 12 months

c) be accompanied on a motorway

d) have valid motor insurance

Answer: D

34. For which of following MUST a driver show his insurance certificate?

a) When making a SORN.

b) When buying or selling a vehicle.

c) When a police officer asks you for it

d) When having an mot inspection

   Answer: C

**35. You will not be able to renew one of these without a
current MOT certificate**

a) Your driving licence

b) Your vehicle insurance

c) Your vehicle excise licence

d) Your vehicle registration document

   Answer: C

**36. The Pass plus Scheme is operated by DVSA for newly
qualified motor vehicle drivers. What is it planned to
achieve?**

a) To improve your basic skills.

b) Reduce the cost of your driving licence.

c) Prevent you from paying congestion charges.

d) Allow you to supervise a learner driver.

   Answer: A

CHAPTER THREE

RULES OF THE ROAD

(39 Questions and Answers)

1. When you are travelling on a motorway in England, you must stop when signalled to do so by which of the following?

a) Flashing amber lights above your lane

b) A traffic officer

c) Pedestrians on the hard shoulder

d) A driver who has broken down

Answer: B

2. Can a driver be allowed to drive over a footpath?

a) To overtake slow-moving traffic

b) When the pavement is very wide

c) If no pedestrians are near

d) To get into a property

Answer: D

3. When are you allowed to drive a motor car in the bus lane shown below?

a)   When the bus is not in its hours of operation

b)   To drive to the front of a traffic queue

c)   You may not use it at any time

d)   To overtake slow-moving traffic

Answer: A

4. **You are driving on a well-lit road at night in a built-up area. By using dipped headlights you will**

a)   see further along the road

b)   go at a much faster speed

c)   switch to main beam quickly

d)   be easily seen by others

Answer: D

5. **You are not allowed to reverse**

a)   for longer than necessary

b)   for more than a car's length

c)   into a side road

d)   in a built-up area

Answer: A

6. **It is pertinent not to stop your vehicle on a clearway**

a)   at any time

b)   when it is busy

c)   in the rush hour

d)   during daylight hours

Answer: A

7.   Which of the following has priority at an unmarked crossroads?

a)   The larger vehicle

b)   No one has priority

c)   The faster vehicle

d)   The smaller vehicle

Answer: B

8.   You are advised to enter a box junction when

a) there are less than two vehicles in front of you

b) the traffic lights show green

c) your exit road is clear

d) you need to turn left

Answer: C

9. **You should not do which of the following when you are looking for a place to park your car, when the only available space is marked 'disabled use'?**

a) use these spaces when elsewhere is full

b) park if you stay with your vehicle

c) use these spaces, disabled or not

d) not park there unless permitted

Answer: D

10. **Where is the most secure place to park your vehicle at night?**

a) In a garage

b) On a busy road

c) In a quiet car park

d) Near a red route

Answer: A

11. **You are not allowed to park**

a) on a one-way street

b) near a police station

c) on a side road

d) near a school entrance

Answer: D

12. **What are you supposed to do if you are parked at a level crossing with a flashing red light even after a train has passed?**

a) Get out and investigate

b) Telephone the signal operator

c) Continue to wait

d) Drive across carefully

Answer: C

13. **What is the speed limit when you are driving on a road that no traffic signs, but there are street lights?**

a) 20 mph

b) 30 mph

c) 40 mph

d) 60 mph

Answer: B

14. **What should you do on approach as you intend to turn left into a minor road?**

a) maintain just left of the middle of the road

b) maintain in the middle of the road

c) swing out wide just before turning

d) continue well to the left of the road

Answer: D

15. **You are travelling along a road that has a cycle lane marked by a solid white line. This implies that during its period of operation**

a) you may park your vehicle on the lane

b) you may move in that lane at any time

c) the lane may be used when it becomes important

d) you must not drive your vehicle in that lane

Answer: D

16. **What is the right hand lane for: on a three-lane dual Carriageway?**

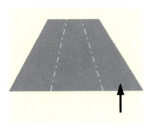

a) overtaking only, never turning right

b) overtaking or turning right

c) fast-moving traffic only

d) turning right only, never overtaking

   Answer: B

17. **What does the below sign represent?**

a) Local speed limit applies

b) No waiting on the carriageway

c) National speed limit applies

d) No entry to vehicular traffic

Answer: C

18. **As a driver, you MUST stop when signalled to do so by one of these**

a) motorcyclist

b) pedestrian

c) police officer

d) bus driver

Answer: C

19. **What does a flashing amber light mean at a pelican crossing?**

a) You must not drive off until the lights stop flashing

b) You must yield to pedestrians still on the crossing

c) You can drive off, even if pedestrians are still on the crossing

d) You must come to a halt because the lights are about to change to red

Answer: B

20. **At toucan crossings, apart from pedestrians, drivers should also be aware of which of these?**

a) emergency vehicles emerging

b) buses pulling out

c) trams crossing in front

d) cyclists riding across

Answer: **D**

21. **When is it advisable for a vehicle driver to reverse from a side road into a main road?**

a) When there are no traffic on both roads

b) Not at any time

c) At any time

d) Only if there are no traffic on the main road

Answer: **B**

22. **You are not allowed to PARK your vehicle**

a) on a roadway with a 40 mile per hour speed limit

b) at a bus stop or very close to it

c) where there is no existence of pavement

d) within 20 metres of a junction

Answer: **B**

23. **When driving straight ahead at a roundabout, you are required to do one of the following**

a) signal left before leaving the roundabout

b) not to signal at any time

c) signal right when approaching the roundabout

d) indicate left when approaching the roundabout

Answer: **A**

24. **What should you do when waiting to cross at a zebra crossing and pedestrians are standing on the pavement?**

a) move on quickly before they step onto the crossing

b) stop your vehicle before you reach the zigzag lines and let them cross

c) stop, let them cross, wait patiently

d) ignore them as they are still on the pavement

Answer: C

25. **When would you use the right-hand lane on a two-lane dual carriageway?**

a) To overtake slower traffic

b) For normal progress

c) When staying at the minimum allowed speed

d) To keep travelling at a steady high speed

Answer: A

26. **Traffic signals are usually given by direction indicators as well as the**

a) brake lights

b) side lights

c) fog lights

d) interior lights

Answer: B

27. When are you required to stop your vehicle?

a) If you are involved in an incident

b) At a junction where there is Give Way line

c) At the end of a one-way street

d) Before merging onto a motorway

Answer: A

28. When would the greatest hazard to passing traffic occur if you are reversing your vehicle into a side road?

a) After you've completed the manoeuvre

b) Just before you actually begin to manoeuvre

c) After you've entered the side road

d) When the front of the vehicle you are travelling in swings out

Answer: D

29. If the dual carriageway you are turning right onto has a very narrow central reservation. What next?

a) Proceed to the central reservation and wait

b) Stay where you are until the road is clear in both directions

c) Stop in the first lane so that other vehicles give way

d) Emerge slightly to show your intentions

Answer: B

30. If your vehicle is parked on the road at night, when must you make use of the sidelights?

a) Where there is an existence of continuous white lines in the middle of the road

b) Where the speed limit exceeds 30 mph

c) Where you are facing oncoming traffic

d) Where you are near a bus stop

Answer: B

31. You may be allowed to wait in a yellow box junction if

a) oncoming traffic is preventing you from turning right

b) you are in a queue of traffic turning left

c) you are in a queue of traffic to go ahead

d) you are on a roundabout

Answer: A

32. **It may be ideal to remove your seat belt when carrying out a manoeuvre that includes**

a) Reversing

b) A hill start

c) An emergency stop

d) Driving slowly

Answer: A

33. **One of the following is what you should have if you MUST park in a disabled Space as shown below**

a) A Blue Badge

b) A wheelchair

c) An advanced driver certificate

d) An adapted vehicle

Answer: A

34. **You want to park and you see a sign showing days and times as shown below. What should you do?**

a) Park your car in a bay and not pay

b) Park on car on yellow lines and pay

c) Park on your car on yellow lines and not pay

d) Park in a bay and pay

Answer: D

35. **What are you supposed to do when there is a car coming towards you, and the road is only wide enough for just one vehicle**

a) Turn into a passing place on your right

b) Make the other driver to reverse

c) Turn into a passing place if your vehicle is wider

d) Turn into a passing place on your left

Answer: D

36. **What are you required to do when entering an area of road works with a temporary speed limit displayed**

a) Not exceed the speed limit

b) Obey the limit only during rush hour

c) Ignore the displayed limit

d) Obey the limit except at night

Answer: A

37. **You are driving on a road that has a cycle lane and the lane is marked by a broken white line. What does that supposed to mean?**

a) you should not drive in the lane unless it is unavoidable

b) That there is a reduced speed limit for vehicles travelling on the lane

c) Cyclists can travel in both directions in that lane

d) The lane must be used by motorcyclists in heavy traffic

Answer: A

38. **You are towing a small caravan on a dual carriageway. You must not exceed**

a) 50 mph

b) 40 mph

c) 70 mph

d) 60 mph

Answer: D

39. At a busy unmarked crossroads, which of the following has priority?

a) Vehicles going straight ahead'

b) Vehicles turning right

c) None of the vehicles

d) The vehicles that arrived first

Answer: C

CHAPTER FOUR

ROAD SIGNS TEST

(43 Questions and Answers)

1. What is the meaning of this sign?

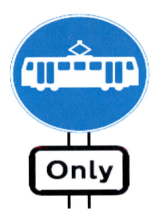

a) Route for trams only

b) Route for buses only

c) Parking for buses only

d) Parking for trams only

Answer: A

2. **What does the below sign mean?**

a) Level crossing with gate or barrier

b) Gated road ahead

c) Level crossing without gate or barrier

d) Cattle grid ahead

Answer: A

3. **What should you do when you are driving on a motorway   and red flashing light appears above your lane, only**

a) Keep moving on that lane and look for further information

b) Drive into another lane in good time

c) Pull over on the shoulder and stop

d) Stop your vehicle and wait for an instruction to proceed

   Answer: B

4. Where are you likely to see a contra flow bus and cycle lane?

a) On a dual carriageway

b) On a roundabout

c) On an urban motorway

d) On a one-way street

   Answer: D

5. What is the meaning of this sign?

a) Cyclists must dismount

b)   Cycles are not allowed

c)   Cycle route ahead

d)   Cycle in single file

   Answer: C

6.   **What is the meaning of the traffic sign shown below?**

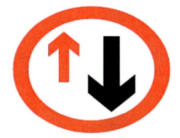

a)   No overtaking allowed

b)   Give priority to oncoming traffic

c)   Two way traffic

d)   One-way traffic only

   Answer: B

7.   **As you are approaching a red traffic light as shown below, what will be the next signal light to show?**

a) Red and amber

b) Green alone

c) Amber alone

d) Green and amber

Answer: A

8. Where would you see this kind of road marking?

a) At traffic lights

b) On road humps

c) Near a level crossing

d) At a box junction

Answer: B

9. What is the meaning of this sign

a) Multi-exit roundabout

b) Risk of ice

c) Six roads converge

d) Place of historical interest

Answer: B

10. What is the meaning of the sign shown below?

a) No footpath

b) No pedestrians

c) Zebra crossing

d) School crossing

Answer: C

11. What does this sign means?

a) tourist attraction

b) beware of trains

c) level crossing

d) beware of trams

Answer: A

12. What is the meaning of this sign?

a) Slippery road ahead

b) Tyres liable to punctures ahead

c) Danger ahead

d) Service area ahead

Answer: C

13. What is the meaning of this sign?

a)   No parking

b)   No road markings

c)   No through road

d)   No entry

Answer: D

14. What does this sign stand for?

a)   Service area 30 miles ahead

b)   Maximum speed 30 mph

c)   Minimum speed 30 mph

d)   Lay-by 30 miles ahead

Answer: B

15. This sign is telling you to

a) follow the route diversion

b) follow the signs to the picnic area

c) give way to pedestrians

d) give way to cyclists

Answer: A

16. What is the meaning of these zigzag lines at pedestrian, as shown below?

a) No parking at any time

b) Parking allowed only for a short time

c) Slow down to 20 mph

d) Sounding horns is not allowed

Answer: A

17. **Which of these shapes is used represents a 'give way' sign?**

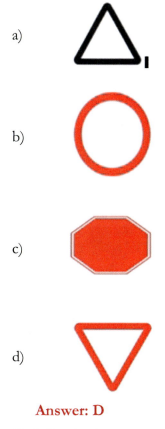

a)

b)

c)

d)

Answer: D

18. **What is the meaning of the sign shown below?**

a) Roundabout

b) Crossroads

c) No stopping

d) No entry

Answer: C

19. **Which of these signs represents 'no entry'?**

a)

b)

c)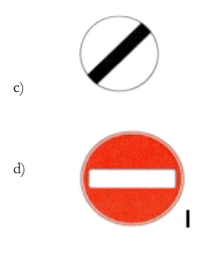

d)

Answer: D

20. What does this sign represents?

a)   Crosswinds

b)   Road noisome

c) Airport

d) Adverse camber

Answer: A

21. **What is the meaning of the motorway sign shown below?**

a) Change to the lane on your left

b) Leave the motorway at the next exit

c) Change to the opposite carriageway

d) Pull up on the hard shoulder

Answer: A

22. **Where would you find these flashing red lights indicating STOP**

a) Pelican crossings

b) Motorway exits

c) Zebra crossings

d) Level crossings

Answer: D

23. What are you required to do when you see this sign?

a) Stop, only if traffic is approaching

b) Stop, even if the road is clear

c) Stop, if children are waiting to cross the road

d) Stop, if a red light is flashing

Answer: B

24. Which place are you likely to see these road markings?

a) At a level crossing

b) On a motorway slip road

c) At a pedestrian crossing

d) On a single-track road

Answer: B

25. What does the below sign represent?

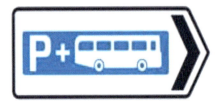

a) Direction to park-and-ride car park

b) No parking for buses or coaches

c) Directions to bus and coach park

d) Parking area for cars and coaches

Answer: A

26. What is the meaning of this overhead signal on a motorway?

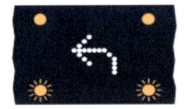

a) Leave the motorway at the next exit

b) All vehicles use the hard shoulder

c) Sharp bend to the left ahead

d) Stop, all lanes ahead closed

Answer: C

27. When you have a white line like this along the centre of the road, it is known as a

a) bus lane marking

b) hazard warning

c) give way marking

d) lane marking

Answer: B

28. Why is it important to cancel your vehicle's indicators after turning?

a) To avoid flattening the battery

b) To avoid misleading other road users

c) To avoid dazzling other road users

d) To avoid damage to the indicator relay

Answer: B

29. Which of these signs means NO motor vehicles permitted?

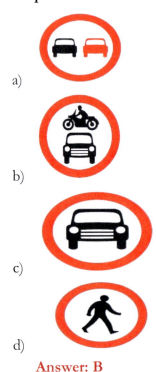

a)

b)

c)

d)

Answer: B

30. What is the meaning of this sign?

a) Through traffic to use left lane

b) Right-hand lane T-junction only

c) Right-hand lane closed ahead

d) 11 tonne weight limit

Answer: C

31. Which of these signs means that you have priority over approaching vehicle?

a)

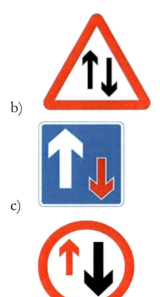

b)

c)

d)

Answer: C

32. What do the following sign mean?

a)   Keep in one lane

b)   Give way to oncoming traffic

c)   Do not overtake

d)   Form two lanes

Answer: C

33. Which of the following signs means 'no stopping'?

a)

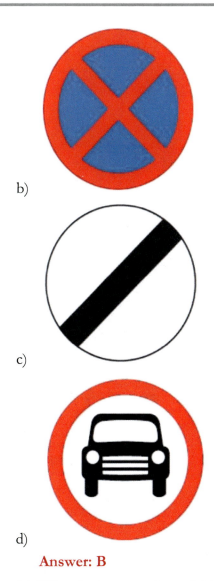

b)

c)

d)

Answer: B

34. What is the meaning of this sign?

a) Uneven road surface

b) Bridge over the road

c) Road ahead ends

d) Water across the road

Answer: D

35. Which of the following sign represents the presence of pedestrians on the road

a)

b)

c)

d)

Answer: A

36. What is the meaning of the below sign?

a) Low bridge ahead

b) Tunnel ahead

c) Ancient monument ahead

d) Traffic danger spot ahead

Answer: B

37. What is the meaning of the sign shown below?

a) Two-way traffic straight ahead

b) Two-way traffic crosses a one-way road

c) Two-way traffic over a bridge

d) Two-way traffic crosses a two-way road

Answer: B

38. What is the meaning of '25' on the motorway sign shown below?

a)   The distance to the nearest town

b)   The route number of the road

c)   The number of the next junction

d)   The speed limit on the slip road

Answer: C

39. What is the meaning of the sign shown below

a)   Crossroads

b)   Level crossing with gate

c)   Level crossing without gate

d)   Ahead only

Answer: A

40. When you sight this amber traffic light as shown below, which other light or lights will come up next?

a) Red alone

b) Red and amber together

c) Green and amber together

d) Green alone

Answer: A

41. What is the meaning of this sign?

a) Turn left for parking area

b) No through road on the left

c) No entry for traffic turning left

d) Turn left for ferry terminal

Answer: B

42. What should you do when you see this sign at a crossroad?

a)   maintain the same speed

b)   carry on with great care

c)   find another route

d)   call the police

Answer: B

43. What is the meaning of this sign?

a)   Maximum speed limit with traffic calming

b)   Minimum speed limit with traffic calming

c)   'Twenty cars only' parking zone

d)   Only twenty cars allowed at any one time

Answer: A

FREQUENTLY ASKED QUESTIONS

What is the minimum age requirement for the tests?

You are eligible to take the theory test when you have attained the age of 17 and above

How can I request for my theory test?

You can request for your test online with the DVSA directly. You should have the following with you

1. UK driving licence number

2. Email address

3. Credit or Debit card

What does the theory tests constitute?

The test has two parts:

a) Multiple-choice questions

b) Hazard perception – this is a video test about spotting hazards on the road

You are required to take them as a single test and must pass both of them to pass the test.

What am I required to study?

You are required to study the under listed:

1. The Highway Code

2. Traffic signs and symbols

3. Essential driving skills

So, the above are what you must study to ensure you know all the rules and skills that will appear in the test. .

Where are these questions from?

The questions are from the DVSA revision question bank.

Made in the USA
Monee, IL
14 September 2023

08427a83-fa51-4ac4-a102-cbf201682321R01